ONE-ACT PLAYS BY
D-MITCH THE POET

One-Act Plays by D-Mitch The Poet

THREE SPOKEN WORD INFUSED INSPIRATIONAL ONE-ACT PLAYS.

Darrell Mitchell II

DM Ink Publishing

Contents

One-Act Plays: Three spoken word infused one-act plays by D-Mitch the poet
Published by DM Ink Publishing House LLC
 Los Angeles, CA
www.DMThePoet.com
678-871-0818
 ISBN: 979-8-9879030-1-8

First Printing, 2023

1

Introduction

This collection of dazzling one-act plays are intriguing, entertaining and they will keep you on the edge of your seat. The short stories are creatively infused with spoken word poems written by Darrell Mitchell II. Laugh out loud with the trial of the century, The State vs D-Mitch The Poet as the jury delivers their controversial verdict. Hold onto your gut and your heart as you fall in love with my therapist has a therapist which is a hilarious romantic comedy. Lastly, you'll enjoy storytelling at its finest with the poet and the secret book which is an inspirational masterpiece.

2

My Therapist has a Therapist

Character List:
The Poet
Therapist
Length:10min
Synopsis: D-Mitch the poet visits his therapist to help him with his emotional intelligence.

Scene 1

THE POET
(The sound of someone knocking at a door, knock, knock, knock)

THERAPIST
Come in

THE POET
Good evening, Dr.

THERAPIST

Good evening Mr. Poet, how are you feeling today?

THE POET

Good question, I'm doing good and feeling even better. How about you?

THERAPIST

I'm well, thanks for asking. Shall we begin our session?

THE POET

Yes, I'm sorry.

THERAPIST

For what?

THE POET

I lied. I'm not doing well; this smile is a mask to cover what's going on inside but that's why I'm here. I want to be mentally & emotionally transparent but it's apparent I still need to work at it. When people ask how you are doing, do they really care? Or is it a set up question to open the door for someone to express how they really feel?

THERAPIST

You're overthinking.

THE POET

What if?

THERAPIST

Don't

THE POET

What if...

THERAPIST

(Blank stare)

THE POET

What if everyone else is underthinking?
Maybe I'm just too demanding.
Maybe I'm just like my father, too bold.
Maybe I'm just like my mother.
She's never satisfied…

THERAPIST

Mr. Poet stop! Well, that's great that you are making steps towards changing and growing. Did you complete the homework assignment?

THE POET

Speaking of homework and steps, I took a lot of them last night, and yes, I did try to complete it, but things got a little crazy.

THERAPIST

How so?

THE POET

Well, I took your advice and I tried to be spontaneous and romantic, so I stood outside of her complex and tossed little pebbles at her window and saying, she loves me, she loves me not, and after the third she loves me not she opened the window and yelled out!

"Go home or I'll call the cops! So, I ran down the block to the bus stop, only to realize that I parked my car in the other direction. And then I noticed a bus drive by with a very large billboard on it that said love. Which inspired me to write this poem.

THE POET

I tried to reach the city of trust through lust,

And ended up in a state of fuss,

Traveling is ruff on the date bus,

So, love me or like me not,

For better or for worse,

Forgive me and hate me not,

But grade me on a relationship curve,

Even though I can get on your very last nerve,

Talk to me not at me like we are equals,

Until you need damage control to reconstruct the mold,

My heart won't sob lonely teardrops,

Because passionate beats get old,

Cold shoulders so silent you can hear a pin drop,

Like this priceless love has been sold,

A vacant sign instead of a heartthrob at the heart break hotel bus stop,

I was in it to win it, from the very first time I bought your ticket

Now I'm glad the love bus runs every fifteen minutes

THERAPIST

Did you notice the red flags?

THE POET

Yes, but I thought it was a carnival.

THERAPIST

You often use humor to deflect trauma.

THE POET

Thank you

THERAPIST

I didn't say it was a good thing.

THE POET

What I'm hearing is that you think I'm funny.

THERAPIST

I have a question? Have you ever heard of the 5 love languages?

THE POET

No, I've never heard of it is there an audiobook or class I can take? I've studied Spanish, French but never love.

THERAPIST

You have to be honest and ask yourself what it is that you respond to, communication is very important.

THE POET

Okay, hey self, yes, what is it that...

THERAPIST

No, I didn't mean it literally. It seems that you fall in love too quickly.

THE POET

What babe?

THERAPIST

Okay use your imagination and visualize meeting the love of your life. The person you would like to spend the rest of your life with.

THE POET

I'm looking for love, have you seen it,
Because I can't find it,
I'm trying to fill this exclusive void inside of me that's oh so elusive,
The truth is,

That I'm so complex communication can be a seesaw conversation,
While speed dates to find soul mates can be like a world cup race,
I'm just a love refugee looking for a heart to call home,
Not to roam or vacation there,
In the middle of the pit of despair,
I want to visit eternity with you and live as if a pair,
Can I occupy your space and share air in an electric atmosphere,
Connecting with fantasy island dreams,
Speechless as I look into your eyes and comprehend what it means
just to relate,
And feel alive, possibly in sync,
Where our differences start our quirky ends meet,
I walked away from love because I didn't know much about it,
Only to search the world to learn that I could live without it,
I took a chance at the game, but I couldn't line up the hearts,
Spinning to win dreams I found out that in order to hit the jackpot,
I have to learn to love myself to start

THERAPIST

Did you think about what it would feel like to fall in love at
first sight?

THE POET

Yes, and I got that warm fuzzy feeling you get inside when you
see their smile. And that's a lot better than getting suspect and sketchy
vibes any day. It was like I was watching a movie. I could see it now...

THE POET

Every day is like another day in paradise,
We are the same like water and ice,
My soul mate which equates to you,
Fulfilling my top ten list of questions by one hundred percent,

What's your passion let's talk about it,
What's your dream let's be about it,
Any problem let me see about it,
Even if the problem stretches out longer than an ostrich neck,
I won't be stressed but blessed by your presence,
Never neglected is what's expected,
You trust I won't act reckless,
But hang tight like a diamond necklace as you sparkle like one.
Your beautiful colorful love rays,
Warm me like the sun,
Woman I crown you queen,
Because you act like one,
Let's combine compromise and despise all haters,
Forming a union everlasting through time distance and temptation,
Me for you and you for me the two musketeers' baby we'll make history,
A legacy, can you picture it.
With no side dames, you're a work of art let me be your frame,
And we can be God's family on earth,
Your worth more than jewel's rubies, or sapphire stones,
Your so precious, our lives were meant to be spiritually sewn together,
Soul mate my soul waits and it's set aside eternally forever,
That's a long time,
But not long enough when you're happy,
Let's slow dance on a fast record,
As life plays out and smile out loud, as our positive synergy,
Creates a love cloud and with that it keeps away the dark one's,
That are light grey in color and filled with lonely days,
Which describes how I feel any time that I spend away from you,
And as I awake from this dream date, my soul mate,
My soul waits for you, to realize who I am to you.

THERAPIST

Very nice, you should share that with others.

Do you think there is anything holding you back from opening yourself up to find true love?

THE POET

Not anymore, I think everyone must deal with heartbreaks and breakups and emotional triggers from the past. But it's all a part of life and how you process it.

THERAPIST

You are correct. Now what do we do when we are sad?

THE POET

Add to cart?

THERAPIST

No

THE POET

Make a voodoo doll?

THERAPIST

Wrong answer

THE POET

Re-download a dating app to feel validated by strangers?

THERAPIST

Absolutely not!

THE POET

Instead of rehearsing fears I want to experience the positive energy that is produced from being a part of a beautiful love story.

THE POET

I've never seen an angel before,
But what now stood before me seemed to be glowing,

And I say to myself, wow she is a natural born wonder,
No fantasy island story just a pretty smile that hit me like thunder,
From the start we would look into each other's eyes,
And hope that neither one of us was anything else in disguise,
I had my doubts that what I felt couldn't of been real,
That's she's actually a good woman and my heart she may steal,
So I put up the wall that was built from past relations,
Bad ones good ones all experiences to learn and grow from,
You just can't let it blur your vision from finding the right one,
Were talking about having a verbal joust,
Trying to find out who will be the first to be knocked out,
Instead we end up in a conversational zone,
Everything disappears and nothing matters except us on the phone,
We exchange views , secrets and dreams,
We talk politics, religion and what life means,
After hours and hours of conversation on the phone,
We fellowship and I read you a poem and from there,
You are the Queen of our home,
I want you ,
Yes you, you make living and loving all worth while,
I need you, yes I do,
I need you connected to me like I need my legs connected to my feet,
Like I need air to breath,
Like a tribe needs a chief. I need you with me,
I like you,
I like you like I like seeing us as kids trying to play in the street,
I like you like seeing Rosa parks on the bus resting in her seat.
Or like seeing Jesus pleased,
I love you,
 I love you like nothing ever before,
I love you like something I will not ever feel again,
I love you like I don't want it to end,
I 'll love you for infinity,

THERAPIST (Snaps both fingers repeatedly)

Snap snap snap out of it. Very good job, I think you are ready to go out and achieve your desires, dreams and much more! As a matter of fact, I think it's time for me to close out this session. With all this talk about love, healing and believing I decided to schedule an appointment with a therapist myself. Have a great day and I'll follow up with you at our next appointment.

THE POET

So, my therapist has a therapist. Very interesting! Enjoy your day doc!

END SCENE

3

The Trial of the Century: The System vs The Poet

Character List:

Defendant: The Poet

Judge Lots of Time

Plaintiff: Counsel (Lawyer)

Bailiff

Jury: Audience

Length: 10min

Synopsis: D-Mitch The poet has been summoned to a court hearing and is being accused of inspiring the youth to follow their dreams.

SCENE 1

BALIFF

Hear Ye! Hear Ye! The court's in session. The system vs The poet. Let's get this show on the road. Everyone rise the honorable Judge lots of time will be preceding over the case. After hearing the closing arguments the jury will give their verdict with faith.

JUDGE LOTS OF TIME

Everybody come to order, let's get this thing in play! Excuse me counsel, did you have something to say?

COUNSEL

Your honor if you please. The defendant is being charged with spreading doubt, using a divisive language and being disruptive. He is a dangerous threat and is very deceptive.

JUDGE LOTS OF TIME

How do you plead

THE POET

I'm Innocent your honor

COUNSEL

Ladies and gentlemen of the jury , your honor too, I think it's quite plain and simple as to what you need to do.
He claims to be the victim, and he claims he is being falsely accused.

THE POET

The evidence is right in front of you, but you can't handle the truth.

COUNSEL

Did you order the code red?

THE POET

Objection your honor!

JUDGE LOTS OF TIME

Sustained! No outburst in this court. Poet what do you have to say about these allegations about spreading doubt.

THE POET

If I told you the truth,

It might scare you to death,

You may not be afraid of life,

But you might be terrified of yourself,

Too full of pride to ask for help,

Seemingly swimming through your sorrows,

Back stroking into tomorrow,

While I surf through life on words,

Like I observe surfers using long boards to ride thru hallowed tidal waves,

Less amazed and more amazing,

I've long understood my short comings,

It's like the second coming of me becoming more in tune with myself,

And going hard in dark trying to follow previously laid successful footsteps,

Like the next level is the only level left,

In a game with no refs,

Life can leave you with no help,

Farfetched until you zoom in closer,

And discover detailed steps that lead off into a ponderosa,

That resembles a field of dreams so I dance amongst the lilies,

From the city to the mountain top and back to the valley,

Wrong words can lead into dead ends and back alleys,

When you politic with colorful communication,

Barriers are a mere abbreviation,

So wait for me on the side of the road at the nearest weigh station,

Where my heavy words weigh a ton, and are heavenly to some,

Your postings and tweets may read that you're winning but my book says I've already won!

COUNSEL

Your honor the defendant claims that you can achieve anything that you put your mind to and he is spreading this hogwash and repeating this gibberish and causing delusional thinking. He is causing people to think outside the box and he must be stopped.

BALIFF

That's a good tweet, I might have to use that.

THE POET

Wasn't it! What's your IG I'll follow you.

COUNSEL

It's lawyergang_boss.

JUDGE LOTS OF TIME

Order in the court!

COUNSEL

The court will now call the poet to the stand

BALIFF

Do you swear to tell the truth, the whole truth about why, what and who? About how it is you do what you do ?

THE POET

For sure Jack!

BALIFF

Right on Brother!

THE POET

I'm constantly, consciously working on my people skills,
I used to ignorantly study space age pimping,
Now I'm watching how folks forget about basic communication,
While your language is deteriorating and your attitude kills,
Can't relate socialize, integrate or talk real,
I was clocked and recorded, typing at seventy-five words per minute,
Now I speak ten times faster and my creativity has no limit,
If this head down worship keeps up,
I predict a lot more people postured, slumped over with a hump,
Thumb tied not tongue tied,
Not able to shake hands or just say hi,

How are you or hello,

Cats communicate the old school way by sending typed notes,

Via super light speeds pony express,

Go ahead be my guest and purposely take this out of context,

If I said the word sea and typed the letter C,

My short hand texting will obliviously leave you lost,

This new age format has people going on internet dates in a chat room with a painted back drop,

Not equipped to simply talk or converse,

Space age communication has me sending verbal's on a high flying first class charter,

These days you would have better luck trying to talk to a fish with no lips underwater.

COUNSEL

I rest my case.

JUDGE LOTS OF TIME

Mr. Poet what do you have to say to these heavy allegations and accusations you've been requested to defend. What's this charge or of creating life with your pen.

THE POET

If I could create life with my pen,

Then I would fill the page with ink droplets,

That will rain down on you,

To wash away a frown or two,

You see light like fire flies,

Flickering underneath and against night skies,

Words sway like stems of wheat,

Resembling how vertical sentences look,

When you look at me sideways after I speak,

Mentioning unmentionables,

Those things we say and don't do,

You dream and don't pursue,
Wake up and take your head out of the noose,
But some refuse the truth,
Instead of being patient and focusing on greatness,
Forever learning so my mind frame is really my time frame,
Incorporating new ways of succeeding,
So I won't go insane repeating useless tactics,
I need that above average strategy,
I use to think I was two words away from being stoned,
Due to making folks mad at me,
Regardless of what's going on under the sun,
I'm not trying to impress anyone,
Just to express one maybe two opinions,
On dominion politics and kingdoms,
Just kidding, I'm fishing can you catch my drift,
I'm swaying on the edge of a cliff,
Flying words like kites,
With plenty wind,
To the heavens they soar with no end,
But when I get it into my mind,
And carve it into my heart,
And speak it out of my mouth,
I let the universe do it's part,
Opposition I hear you listening,
See you watching, I know you plotting,
But there is no dimming Gods lightening like glow,
If I could create life with my pen I would begin with the end and open with a close.

JUDGE LOTS OF TIME

Well we have heard both sides, arguments and facts delivered with precision. After hearing from the jury I will announce my decision.

JURY

The jury representative hands the judge a card with the verdict.

JUDGE LOTS OF TIME

Not guilty! Court adjourned!

COUNSEL

(Throws hands up in frustration)

THE POET

(The Poet jumps up out of his chair and celebrates!)

END SCENE

4

The Poet and the Secret Book

Character List:

The Poet

Length: 10min

Synopsis - The poet shares a story of the time when him and his best friend hip hop were inspired by a woman and a mysterious book.

SCENE 1

THE POET

Hello, My name is D-Mitch the Poet and I have the pleasure of sharing with you one of the greatest stories ever told of me and my friend hip hop. One day while at the intersection of inspiration highway and destiny Blvd. Hip hop and I stopped off at the local taco spot, to grab a bite to eat. I was considered a deep thinker and intellectual and hip hop had the fresh style and the witty metaphors. We are both products of our parents, society, and ancestors.

I believe it was fall or maybe winter. It right around the time that we had to change the time back an hour on our clocks. I remember because it started to get darker a little earlier than usual. My friend and

I were walking home from basketball practice. And we talked about everything from life, art and shoes to soul music, dreams, and our daily blues.

Those conversations can get very profound as we walk through town, which made for great practice because we could practice out loud. Minus the sirens in the background, and neighborhood hounds and clowns that would wonder around. Like clockwork hip hop hit me with a freestyle verse and I responded with a poem I had just written called generational curse.

THE POET

Born into sin through a generational curse,

Permanently tattooed with this work since birth,

Feeling like I'm called to sow seeds into the earth while my roots run deep,

So crisscrossed their twisted,

The only thing that was left on my family tree was secrets and old slave pictures,

I came about from things done in the dark,

Now I shine my light through this form of art,

I had an inheritance but I sold my wings for a shiny ring and gave away my kingdom for a slave mentality,

Just to get a starring role in a show called that's my reality,

After hitting rock bottom I found out that I don't need stilts to stand on my own two feet,

Even when the stress is waist deep,

Now I understand I can't live peacefully knowing if I abandon my seeds for a fake dream,

More like a collage of mirages is what it seems,

Originally created out of lies and deceit now I over flow with the truth that was planted inside me deep,

So now the world thinks I'm fifty one fifty , half me, half God plus an earth full of hurt,

The pressure was needed to sprout potential and stop this generational curse,

We kept walking up the street and as we were approaching the crosswalk. My attention turned towards an older lady at the stop light with a scarf wrapped around her head like a hood so you could not see her face. Now, my friend and I are deep in conversation but as we get closer to the corner. I start to realize that the lady has not crossed the street yet.

At first I didn't pay it any mind. After we reach the lady I ask her if she needs help crossing the street. She didn't look up at me, she just nodded her head twice. As we walked side by side I walked a little bit slower than normal to make sure she could keep up with the pace. She wore this long wool jacket that went down to her ankles, I couldn't really see her feet moving so she seemed to be gliding.

After crossing the crosswalk, I say okay have a good day. She mumbled something but I couldn't hear what she was saying so I bent down to hear her better. But I still couldn't hear her or see her face so I got a little closer, At that moment I heard a loud growl! Grrrrrr!

My friend growled and grabs my shoulder laughing at my response. Startled and shocked I turn to my friend and say what. He say's the light is green let's go. I said okay and turn back around to say good bye to the lady but she was already halfway up the block.

For a senior she sure did walk fast. Then I noticed an old diary looking book with an incredibly amazing design embroidered on the cover. The lady must of dropped it so I look up in the direction she was walking to say hey you forgot this and she was gone.

Hip hop and I noticed the book on the ground at the same time and we both reached to pick it up. I had the front cover in my hand and he had the back cover in his. Neither of us would let go and as we pulled back and forth, until the book tore into two pieces! I noticed that there was a book marker that was sticking out from one of the pages of the book. I opened the page and there was a handwritten poem and I turn to my friend and I say hey check this out.

THE POET

I wake up trying to recall my dreams from last night,
So important like they held the meaning to my life,
Expectation flies high and hope anchors my soul,
Collecting flash backs as the day goes by,
Piecing together scenes, symbolic themes pass by posing,
For pictures my mind has already taken,
Properly aligned destiny is the destination,
Speaking to me from a place expressed thru my imagination,
I dream of dreams using life to translate what they mean,
Every night until the light breaks I consistently chase my dreams,

THE POET

He turns to me and says did you write that? I said no not at all. It was already written. With a surprised expression, we look at each and say Freaky Friday! I'm almost home now and this is were I walk the last block home alone. Hip hop goes his way and I go mine. As I'm passing the convenience store parking lot I notice this warmth and brightness out the corner of my eye. I look up and notice that it is a mural and to my surprise it resembles the lady that I helped cross the street.

I immediately see an artist touching up a corner of the painting. I walk over and asked her who the person on the wall is. She began to tell me of a story of an old writer that used to live in the area. She said it's an old myth but as the story goes she wonders the area waiting for someone to go a good deed for her. Once the deed is done, she vanishes and usually leaves a gift. It's been called a gift because it has to do with the good samaritans dreams and desires. I stood there in amazement and astonishment. My jaw hit the floor.

I couldn't stay longer and ask more questions because it was getting dark and I had one more block to go. This was my favorite part of the walk home because I got a chance to walk by a lake. There was a hill that I loved to sit on and skip rocks across the water. I decided to stop for a minute and flip through the book to see if there were any more writings. I always loved creativity and short stories but to my surprise page after page was blank. I went through the book until I came to the last page which read.

THE POET

The truth is, deep down in my heart,
Forces of life flow thru channels,
That get formed into a life force powerful enough to fill the canals of my heart,
In order to dock at my harbor,
Sometimes supported by peers, bombarded by info,
I have to be diligent and guard the gate to my ears,
Fear follows doubt constantly trying to reside in my mind,
Debris polluting the sea of possibilities like oil slicks,
Making the hear sick like lonely and bitterness.
But I play the gatekeeper,
Restraining my brain from entertaining the fiery darts of negativity,
I put a mirror to my heart only to find out that I'm harboring my worst enemy,
So I flood my mind, body and soul and overcome it with love,
Engulfing my entire being in joy,
Happiness is a by product so I play with it like a toy,
I'm always on the look out for new things to feed this dream machine,
In order to fill the scene with visions of victory,
Spread the word seed like Johnny apple seed,
Flushing out the misery,
And inspire thoughts that can change history,
All to the beat of drum,
Life sounds like music,
The truth is, how astounding is it that we have a heart that can move mountains!

THE POET

After that I noticed that it was night fall because I could see the reflection of the stars from the sky in the lake. I then picked up a rock and tossed it in the lake right where the star was. As I looked onto the silhouette in the water it began to take shape. It resembled the image of the lady with the scarf. The star became the twinkle in her eye and then she winked at me. I looked down to grab my cell phone and when I looked up to take a picture, the image was gone. I couldn't believe my eyes and immediately called by best friend to tell him what happened. He said he had gone through the same thing and ever since we have been writing nonstop. The greatest story ever told of how a sweet old lady inspired poetry and hip hop.

END SCENE

Darrell Mitchell II endeavors to encourage a generation to think better, write better and live better in life. As an organization we promote thinking on a creative level and assist with various aspects of performing arts through fundraising events, workshops, showcases and community outreach programs. With over 20 books published, and over 100 pieces of artwork and four theater plays. Our goal is to inspire, empower and enlighten the world through art and literature.

Our brand represents products that readers can easily relate to. The current catalog has built a solid foundation among readers and music enthusiast, who currently read and listens to inspirational, empowering and enlightening material. The spoken word poetry collection creates a connection with the reader. This collection also enlightens the reader and provides them with understanding. Each published piece is embedded with a message that challenges the reader to make a connection between ideas and concepts. More importantly, the series of poems give a testimony and explains how you can achieve your dreams by believing in them.